FROM BIG BANDS TO RAP

Contents

Written by Murray Pile

What Is Music?

Music can be powerful. It can make people laugh. It can make them cry. It can make them dance and clap their hands. It can make people think of a special time. It can paint a picture in a person's mind. Music is about sounds. It has three basic features – melody, rhythm, and harmony. All music must have at least one of these things. The words of a song try to tell a story.

Can you explain what the word *music* means? It is not easy. Yet most people in other parts of the world can decide whether or not a sound is musical. Each culture or country has its own sound. But people in India might not like the music from China. And people from China may not like Indian music.

hollow, wooden head

Maracas

Something within a country or culture can affect music. War can inspire protest songs. Songs often praise a famous person and a deed they have performed.

This book includes a timeline. A timeline gives more information about a certain period in time.

The History of Music

Long ago, music was used to praise a birth or to mourn a death. It was used to inspire an army before fighting. It was used as a warning of danger. It was a chant for hunting. It could be used to relax and entertain people.

Ancient music was made by beating out rhythms on drums. Drums were made of animal skins stretched over hollow logs. Twanging the strings on hunting bows made music. Rattling seeds in dried seedpods or seashells was music. Music was made by blowing flutes made of reeds and hollow bones. It was made by playing trumpets made from animal horns or large seashells. It was made by scraping bones with a stick. People also made music without instruments. They chanted, clapped their hands, and whistled.

Dancing to music

Aborigine playing the didgeridoo

1900–1919

In the early 1900s, a lot of people were poor and worked hard to make ends meet. People did not have much time for fun. For a lot of people, music was their only fun. America had two main types of music at the time – ragtime and blues.

Ragtime music came from the cotton plantations in the American south and from cakewalks. The cakewalk was a marching dance performed by African Americans. Contests were held and the winner would get a piece of cake. Big bands performed most of the music.

Blues singing was also shaped by African Americans. It told of their day-to-day life working on the land. Blues musicians played the guitar and the harmonica.

In England in the 1900s, the music hall was a place the poor people visited to be entertained. Music halls started in the bars of London and other big cities. Singers, comedians, dancers, and other entertainers liked to perform in music halls. There were a lot of popular singers during that time.

bc

cov

sour

mout

Harmonica

1903 Bing Crosby born

1900

1901 Louis Armstrong born

Huddie (Leadbelly) Ledbetter

Huddie Ledbetter was an African-American singer. He was also known as Leadbelly. As a teenager in the early 1900s he lived in the Deep South. He played the guitar and sang songs. He had a distinctive voice. He sang about what life was like for poor African Americans.

Over the next 15 years he recorded hundreds of songs. His biggest hit during his lifetime was "Goodnight Irene."

Leadbelly's music has influenced a lot of other great singers and musicians. Leadbelly started his recording career in 1934.

Gracie Fields

Gracie Fields was born in England in 1898. As a child, she was encouraged by her mother to go on the stage. She was a good singer. At an early age, Fields toured around England performing at music halls. She sang on the radio. She made records and worked in film and television. Singers like Fields became stars and were loved by people. The music halls were less popular when radio and motion pictures became popular.

Gracie Fields sang in music halls.

1915 Frank Sinatra born

1917 Duke Ellington forms The Serenaders

1920

1919 First million-selling record "Japanese Sandman" released

1920–1929

flared bell

This period, called the "Roaring 20s," was a time of great social change – in everything from fashion to politics. It was a time of rebuilding for countries involved in World War I. It was an age of wealth. A lot of inventions became popular. These included the radio, the car, and motion pictures.

The popular dance of the 1920s was the Charleston. The Charleston could be danced by one person or with a partner. It could even be danced in a group. It was a dance with a lot of kicks. It had a lot of movements of the arms, hands, and legs.

Jazz was the music of the day. African-American musicians like Bessie Smith, Louis Armstrong, and Duke Ellington made their names in this era. Early on, their records were popular with both black and white people. They played the trumpet and saxophone. Country and western music also became popular in the 1920s.

piston valve

Trumpet

cup-shaped mouthpiece

1923 Birth of Hank Williams Sr.

1920

1923 Bessie Smith releases her first record, "Down-Hearted Blues"

Bessie Smith

Bessie Smith was one of the most popular blues singers of the 1920s. She sold hundreds of thousands of records. Smith earned up to US$2,000 each week. In the 1920s US$2,000 was a lot of money. Smith was also known as the "Empress of the Blues." She was inducted to the Blues Foundation's Hall of Fame in 1980 and the Rock and Roll Hall of Fame in 1989.

Bessie Smith – Empress of the Blues

Louis Armstrong

Louis Armstrong, also known as Satchmo, was a trumpet player. He was also a singer and a bandleader. He was a popular entertainer from the 1920s until he died in 1971.

Like a lot of other musicians, he overcame poverty. He became a star performer who influenced jazz music. He played with a lot of great bands until he formed his own band called Louis Armstrong's Hot Five in 1925.

In New Orleans, a statue was erected and a park named after him. His home in Queens in New York City has been turned into a museum.

Louis Armstrong was a huge influence on jazz.

Duke Ellington

Duke Ellington was a jazz composer, bandleader, and pianist. He is recognized as one of the best composers of jazz. He is also one of the great musicians of the twentieth century. He composed more than 2,000 pieces of music. These included ballets, film scores, musical shows, an opera, and a lot of other music pieces.

Ellington started playing the piano as a teenager. He played for friends and at parties. Soon after, he started his own band. He called the band The Duke's Serenaders.

Because of the fame he achieved as a musician, Ellington was given a lot of awards. These included 11 Grammy Awards, and 19 honorary doctorate degrees. He also received the American Presidential Medal of Freedom. France gave him the Legion of Honor.

Duke Ellington led his own orchestra.

1930–1939

The 1930s were the time of the Great Depression. This was a time when a lot of businesses went bust. Many rich people became poor. The songs of the day showed how the people were feeling. People were not happy because they were out of work, or their wages were cut. Popular songs included "I've Got Five Dollars" and "Brother, Can You Spare a Dime?"

The 1930s were also the start of swing music. Swing was made up of part New Orleans jazz and part big-band music. Swing music and jazz meant a lot of people visited live clubs and dance floors. The radio was also becoming a popular way to listen and dance to music.

The dance of the 1930s was the jitterbug. The jitterbug was danced by couples and was very energetic and popular.

Instruments used during the 1930s included the piano and banjo. The clarinet was a popular instrument in the big bands of the era.

st

banjo

b

Banjo

tail piece

1930

1931 Birth of soul legend Sam Cooke

1935 Birth of Elvis Presle

1936 Louis A

Bing Crosby

Harry Lillis Crosby was born in Tacoma, Washington, in 1903. At high school he started singing jazz. He carried on singing when he went to college in Spokane, Washington. He left college to try and make a career in show business. He thought he could make it as a singer. And he did.

As Bing Crosby, he became one of the most popular singers of all time. The sales of his records were higher than those of any other singer in his era. By the end of the 1930s he was one of the biggest stars in the world. Crosby also starred in a lot of films.

Bing Crosby started out singing jazz.

1938 Ella Fitzgerald releases "A-Tisket, A-Tasket"

1939

"Pennies from Heaven"

1937 Bessie Smith dies

1940–1949

By 1940, World War II had started. It began influencing music. At the time, Vera Lynn was singing "The White Cliffs of Dover" and "There Will Always Be an England," and Marlene Dietrich sang "Lili Marlene."

Big bands with solo singers became popular. These included bands led by Benny Goodman, Glen Miller, Harry James, and Tommy Dorsey. These bands entertained people during World War II. Musicians liked to play the drums, the piano, and clarinet.

After the war, romantic crooners became popular. These were singers such as Frankie Laine, Perry Como, Tony Bennett, Dean Martin, and Rosemary Clooney. This was also the time of the first true pop stars like Frank Sinatra, who would be mobbed by their fans.

mouth

wo
cyli

Clarinet

flared

1940 Woody Guthrie releases "This Land Is Your Land"

1940 Birth of John Lennon

1942 Bing Crosby releases "White Christm

1940

1941 Frank Sinatra's "This Love of Mine" spends 13 weeks at number

Frank Sinatra

Francis Albert Sinatra was born in Hoboken, New Jersey, in 1915. He went on to become one of the most famous singers in the world. Sinatra started his singing career with the big bands when he was in his early twenties.

When Sinatra started to sing as a soloist he copied the singing style of Bing Crosby. Sinatra soon became an idol for teenagers. They swooned over his crooning voice. He also became a film star. His career stretched over six decades.

A young Frank Sinatra ready to sing

1947 Birth of Elton John

1949

1950–1959

In the 1950s, a lot of music began to be written and played for teenagers. Chuck Berry was the first songwriter to write songs in words that young people used. He wrote about things that teenagers cared about. His music was written about rebellion, school, romance, cars, and other things that interested teenagers of the era. Other singers and groups of the age were Bill Haley and the Comets, Buddy Holly, and Elvis Presley.

lar flare

narr conica

Horn

finger key

1953 Hank Williams Sr. dies

1950

1954 Elvis begins recording at Sun Studios

Bill Haley and the Comets

Bill Haley started out as a singer with his band The Saddlemen. They performed country and western songs. They wore cowboy boots, hats, and neck scarves.

The Saddlemen changed their name to the Comets. Their song "Rock Around the Clock" made Bill Haley and the Comets famous in America, Britain, and Australia.

Fans would soon leave Bill Haley and turn their attention to Elvis Presley. Presley dressed and acted more like a teenager.

Later, Bill Haley and the Comets wrote and sang songs for older people. The songs were not as popular. The band broke up and stopped playing. Haley's earlier songs, including "Shake, Rattle, and Roll," "Rock Around the Clock," and "See You Later Alligator," are still popular and sung today.

Bill Haley's fame was brief.

Elvis Presley

Nicknamed the "King of Rock and Roll," Elvis Presley was one of the biggest-selling singers of the twentieth century.

Elvis Aaron Presley was born in Tupelo, Mississippi. At the age of ten he won a talent contest. He sang the country and western ballad "Old Shep." He and his parents moved to Memphis, Tennessee. This is where he spent his teenage years. He recorded "Jailhouse Rock," which became a hit. Elvis was good looking and wore rebellious clothes. He became a teen idol. When he sang, his whole body shook. The crowd would go wild. Soon, he became known simply as Elvis.

Elvis had an amazing 28 hit songs from 1956 to 1972. His hits included "Love Me Tender" and "Don't Be Cruel." He also became a movie star. He was in more than ten movies between 1956 and 1968.

By the 1970s Elvis had become withdrawn and would stay in his mansion known as Graceland. After his death in 1977, some fans would not believe that he was dead. There were a lot of people who reported seeing him alive.

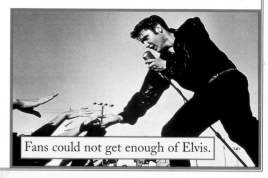

Fans could not get enough of Elvis.

Buddy Holly and the Crickets

Between 1957 and 1959, Buddy Holly was one of the most popular rock-and-roll stars. He sold millions of records.

Holly loved music from a young age. While at school he had his own radio show. Holly and his friends formed a band called the Crickets. They would play and sing at local school functions and parties. They became popular and Holly was offered a recording contract. He and his drummer Jerry Allison wrote the hit song "That'll Be the Day." It became a number one hit.

Buddy Holly and the Crickets went on tour in America with other rock-and-roll stars. These stars included Holly's rock-and-roll friends J. P. "The Big Bopper" Richardson and Ritchie Valens. Before his death in a plane crash in 1959, Holly had five hit songs. These hits included songs such as "Maybe Baby," "Oh Boy," and "Peggy Sue." Even now there is a stage show of Holly's life.

Buddy Holly (second left) was 22 when he died.

1960–1969

The 1960s started out as a time of innocence. There was hope for the future. This hope could be heard in the music. However, the end of the 1960s was a time of great change. Some of this change was because of the war in Vietnam.

Young people known as "hippies" began influencing music. They liked songs that were protesting against the Vietnam War. They urged peace and "flower power." They urged people to look after the planet.

Folk-song singers like Joan Baez, Bob Dylan, and Peter Seeger were well liked. There were also a lot of groups writing their own hit songs. Rock and roll was popular, too. Other bands and singers that people liked listening to were The Beatles, The Rolling Stones, The Beach Boys, The Hollies, The Four Tops, Manfred Mann, and Janis Joplin.

soun

h

Acoustic guitar

hollow

1961 The Beatles first perform at the Cavern Club

1960

1963 Birth of Whitney Houston

The Beatles

The Beatles were the first rock-and-roll band to become superstars. Four young men from Liverpool, England formed the group. It became the most famous band in the world.

The Beatles were guitarists George Harrison and John Lennon, bassist Paul McCartney, and drummer Ringo Starr. They tried things in their recordings that no one had tried before. An example is their song "All You Need Is Love" recorded in 1967. The song included bits of the French national anthem. There were parts by the classical composer Johann Sebastian Bach. There were also other sounds from Beatles' songs.

After a lot of hit songs, the Beatles broke up in 1970. Each member wanted a separate musical career. In 1980, Lennon was shot and killed outside his apartment in New York City. George Harrison died of cancer in November 2001.

The Beatles at the height of their fame

54 Sam Cooke dies

1967 The Beatles release *Sgt. Peppers* album

1966 The Beach Boys release *Pet Sounds* album

1969

The Rolling Stones

Brian Jones, Charlie Watts, Bill Wyman, Mick Jagger, and Keith Richards were the five British musicians who formed The Rolling Stones.

The Beatles were well dressed on and off stage and had tidy haircuts. Most parents thought The Rolling Stones were loud, rude, and untidy. Their music was loud and raw. Young people loved their music. They had a lot of fans. Hit songs included "Satisfaction," "Honky Tonk Woman," and "Miss You."

The Rolling Stones have been performing for more than 35 years.

The Beach Boys

Brian, Carl, and Dennis Wilson were joined by their cousin Mike Love and friend Al Jardine to form The Beach Boys. They started the Californian sound. The Californian sound was also known as surf music.

Surf music became popular throughout the 1960s. Dennis was the only band member who surfed. The others embraced the lifestyle. Brian was the musical genius behind the band. He wrote songs that blended easy-listening melodies with three- or four-part harmonies.

By the early 1970s, The Beach Boys' popularity had dropped. The group began to drift apart. Dennis Wilson drowned off the Californian coast in 1983. Then, in 1988 the group was elected to the Rock and Roll Hall of Fame. Carl Wilson died in 1998 of lung cancer.

The Beach Boys had big hits in the 1960s.

Janis Joplin

Growing up in Texas, Janis Joplin was an unhappy child. Her classmates laughed at her. They made fun of the way she looked and acted. But she found an outlet for her unhappiness in music. After leaving Lamar University in Texas, she joined the Big Brother and the Holding Company band.

Janis playing to the crowd

All the hurt and pain that she had gone through as a child came out in her singing. Joplin's powerful voice won her a lot of fans.

Later she went solo. She took one of the guitarists from the Big Brother and the Holding Company band with her. Joplin died in 1970 at the young age of 27.

1970 Elton John releases "Your Song"

1970

1974 Duke Ellington dies

1970–1979

In the 1970s, the Vietnam War was still raging. There were a lot of changes happening in different countries. Britain had its first female prime minister, Margaret Thatcher. The United States' president Richard Nixon left office in disgrace. New technologies were developed. It was the decade that the Concorde started flying.

Popular music of the 1970s included artists such as Chicago, The Who, Bob Marley, The Jam, Abba, David Bowie, Eric Clapton, Fleetwood Mac, The Eagles, Elton John, Rod Stewart, AC/DC, Led Zeppelin, and The Bee Gees.

In the 1970s, albums became an important part of the music business. It was no longer enough to have a hit single. Fans wanted value for their money. The only way artists could compete was by making albums full of great songs.

The 1970s was also the time of disco, punk rock, and "bubblegum" music. Punk rock gave bands like The Sex Pistols and their fans a way to ask for social change using music.

l wood →

m sticks

taper →

← acorn

The Eagles release *Hotel California* album

1977 Elvis Presley dies

1977 Fleetwood Mac release *Rumors* album

1979

23

The Eagles

The Eagles became one of the biggest-selling rock-music bands in the 1970s. Glenn Frey and Don Henley formed the group in 1971. They were both playing in singer Linda Ronstadt's backing band. Bass player Randy Meisner and guitarist Bernie Leadon joined the band. Later on, Don Felder also became a member. Leadon left The Eagles and was replaced by Joe Walsh. It was during this time that they had their biggest hits. These included the albums *Hotel California* and *The Long Run*. During the 1970s The Eagles had a lot of hit songs including "Desperado," and "New Kid in Town."

The Bee Gees

The Bee Gees are a group made up of brothers Barry, Robin, and Maurice Gibb. They were born in Britain. Their first public show took place when twins Maurice and Robin were seven years old. The Gibb family then went to live in Australia. In Australia the brothers became known as a trio.

To become stars the brothers went back to Britain. It was there they recorded "New York Mining Disaster, 1941." It was their first top-20 single in both America and Britain. In 1977 the Bee Gees released the album *Saturday Night Fever*. It was for a movie of the same name. It went on to become one of the biggest-selling soundtrack albums in the world.

Elton John

Elton John was born in London in 1947 as Reginald Kenneth Dwight. He started his career as a piano-playing singer. He then teamed up with songwriter Bernie Taupin. John and Taupin stopped working together during the late 1970s and 1980s. They started working together again in the 1990s.

John became known for his off-the-wall stage costumes. These included his US$40,000 rose-tinted glasses with diamonds. He also had two-foot (0.7 m) platform shoes. He also liked sequinned jump suits and pink scarves.

His hits included "Crocodile Rock," "Your Song," and "Goodbye Yellow Brick Road." John was inducted into the Rock and Roll Hall of Fame in 1994. In 1995 he won an Academy Award for the song "Can You Feel the Love Tonight?" The song was from the film *The Lion King*.

Elton John is a piano-playing singer.

1980–1989

The music of the 1980s introduced synthesizers. Electronic music had arrived. Compact discs (CDs) became the preferred medium for buying music. They replaced vinyl. In some cases they also replaced cassette tapes. CDs are more durable. They also have a high quality of sound.

Audiences had grown tired of the punk-rock sounds. A lot of people were going back to soul, rock, and rhythm and blues.

As the 1980s drew to a close, a new style of music was becoming popular – rap. Rap featured spoken poems. It also had a heavy beat. Music videos became very popular. The videos allowed recording artists to make their songs into short movies.

Many singers and bands became popular in the 1980s. Bands and singers included REM, Prince, Madonna, Bruce Springsteen, U2, Michael Jackson, and Billy Idol.

Electric guitar

output s

1980 Beatle John Lennon dies   **1984** Madonna releases "Like a Virgin"

1980

1982 Michael Jackson releases *Thriller* album

Michael Jackson

Michael Joseph Jackson was born in Gary, Indiana in 1958. At the age of five he joined four of his brothers. They became known as the Jackson 5.

Jackson was not only a good singer but was also a good dancer. He was soon the star of the group. He left the Jackson 5 to sing and dance on his own.

He recorded a lot of albums. These albums included *Off the Wall*, *Thriller*, and *Dangerous*. His many popular songs include "Beat It," "Billie Jean," and "Bad." Jackson became one of the most famous people in the world. He had an amusement park built at his Neverland ranch in California.

Michael Jackson dancing on stage

1986-87 Whitney Houston has seven consecutive number one hits

1989

84 Bruce Springsteen releases *Born in the USA* album

Madonna

Madonna Louise Veronica Ciccone was born in Bay City, Michigan in 1958. She is now known simply as Madonna.

As a young child, Madonna started acting and dancing lessons. After she left high school she won a dance scholarship to college. After two years, Madonna dropped out. She wanted to start a music career in New York City. She formed a band. She performed songs such as "Holiday," "Material Girl," and "Crazy for You."

The showing of her music videos on MTV helped make her a star. Madonna also liked acting. She won a Golden Globe Award for her part as Eva Peron in the film *Evita*. She also appeared in the hit film *Desperately Seeking Susan*.

Madonna is full of energy during concerts.

1990 Sammy Davis Jr. dies

1990 Public Enemy release *Fear of a Black Planet* album

1990

1991 Nirvana release *Nevermind* album

1990–1999

As in the 1980s, in the 1990s many different types of music were popular. They included country music from stars like Shania Twain. Also popular were boy and girl bands like N'Sync and the Spice Girls.

Another type of music that became well liked during this decade was the music from dance clubs. There were many types of dance music including house and garage music. This music started in Chicago and was influenced by the disco music of the 1970s. Even disc jockeys were becoming pop celebrities. Rap was still popular in the 1990s. Artists such as Queen Latifah and the Beastie Boys sold a lot of records. Others, like Public Enemy, sang songs that had strong social messages.

A new type of music called grunge also started becoming popular. It started in Seattle, Washington. It was epitomized by such bands as Nirvana and Pearl Jam.

Queen Latifah

1997 Spice Girls release *Spice World* album

1999

1998 Frank Sinatra dies

Britney Spears

Britney Jean Spears was born in 1981, in Kentwood, Louisiana. By the age of 11 she was a member of the cast of the television series called the "Mickey Mouse Club."

At seventeen she shot to fame with the release of her first album *Baby One More Time*.

Her success did not stop there. Her second album titled *Oops... I Did It Again*, was just as popular. This album sold more than 1.3 million copies in its first week.

Britney Spears loves performing.

2000 3.6 million copies of The Beatles *1* album sold in one week

2000

2001 Beatle George Harrison dies

Spice Girls

Geri Halliwell, Victoria Adams, Emma Bunton, Melanie Brown, and Melanie Chisholm – better known as Ginger, Posh, Baby, Scary, and Sporty – were the Spice Girls. In 1997 they were the top-selling group in the United States. They sold 5.3 million copies of the album *Spice*.

In 1998, Halliwell left the group to have a solo career. The group decided to continue without her. They remained at the top of the charts. They also received awards for best group and best new pop album at the MTV Europe Music Video Awards. By 2001 the group had split up. Each of the group members started their own solo careers.

The Spice Girls have all gone solo.

All the musicians listed here have been famous and helped influence the music of the past 100 years.

There are a lot more that could have been written about in this book. Not everyone likes the same music and that is why there are so many types of music.

Even though styles and artists change, music continues to inspire, entertain, and feed people's creativity.

Index